365 Days Of Love Quotes:
A Year Of Daily Love, Happiness and Wellbeing.

Barclay Hansen

Content Page

Free Gift

As a thank you for purchasing this book I would like to give you a free gift. It is my PDF action guide titled Beginners Guide To Affirmations: Everything You Need TO Get Started With Affirmations. It is a quick read and is perfect for anyone that wants to start improving their life with affirmations, inside I cover the basics of affirmations, Affirmative Prayer, Cosmic Ordering, Creative Visualization, Mantras and How to build your positive mindset.

https://lifeaffirmations.net/free-gift

Introduction

Love quotes are the perfect way to start the day and set you up for a day of wellbeing and happiness. Inside the pages of this book you will find a range of quotes to give you a daily dose of Love, Happiness, Wellbeing and Hopefulness.

Use this book to start your day on the right foot, to fill you with happiness before bed or any time during the day when you need a boost of hopefulness to help you succeed with whatever the day throws at you.

No matter the circumstance you find yourself in we have quotes to pick you up or keep you motivated to be the best version of yourself.

Quotes

#1
The Best And Most Beautiful Things In The World Cannot Be Seen Nor Even Touched, But Only Just Felt In The Heart.

#2
To Love One Person Among This World's Many And To Have Loved Each Other Deeply For A Long While Is Beautiful.

#3
When You Realize You Want To Spend The Rest Of Your Life With Somebody, You Want The Rest Of Your Life To Start As Soon As Possible.

#4
The Greatest Thing You'll Ever Learn Is Just To Love And Be Loved In Return.

#5
When The Power Of Love Overcomes The Love Of Power The World Will Know Peace.

#6

Sometimes The Heart Sees What Is Invisible
To The Eye.

#7

Laugh As Much As You Breathe And Love As
Long As You Live.

#8

Anyone Can Love A Rose, But It Takes A Lot
To Love A Leaf.

#9

Love Is Like War: Easy To Begin But Very
Hard To Stop.

#10

Real Love Doesn't Meet You At Your Best. It
Meets You In Your Mess.

#11
The Greatest Happiness Of Life Is The
Conviction That We Are Loved; Loved For
Ourselves, Or Rather, Loved In Spite Of
Ourselves.

#12
Love Doesn't Need A Reason. It Speaks From
The Irrational Wisdom Of The Heart.

#13
You Don't Marry Someone You Can Live With
– You Marry The Person Who You Cannot
Live Without.

#14
For Some People, 'The Point Of No Return'
Begins At The Very Moment Their Souls
Become Aware Of Each Other's Existence.

#15
Love Is The Condition In Which The
Happiness Of Another Person Is Essential To
Your Own.

#16
There Is Always Some Madness In Love. But
There Is Also Always Some Reason In
Madness.

#17
There Is Only One Happiness In This Life, To
Love And Be Loved.

#18
True Love Is Rare, And It's The Only Thing
That Gives Life Real Meaning.

#19
They Invented Hugs To Let People Know You
Love Them Without Saying Anything.

#20
Love Is Just A Word Until Someone Comes
Along And Gives It Meaning.

#21
A Simple 'I Love You' Means More Than
Money.

#22
You Don't Love Someone For Their Looks, Or Their Clothes, Or For Their Fancy Car, But Because They Sing A Song Only You Can Hear.

#23
Love Is Absolute Loyalty. People Fade, Looks Fade, But Loyalty Never Fades. You Can Depend So Much On Certain People; You Can Set Your Watch By Them. And That's Love, Even If It Doesn't Seem Very Exciting.

#24
It's Easy To Fall In Love. The Hard Part Is Finding Someone To Catch You.

#25
Pleasure Of Love Lasts But A Moment. Pain Of Love Lasts A Lifetime.

#26
To Lose Balance Sometimes For Love Is Part Of Living A Balanced Life.

#27
Love Is Just A Word, But You Bring It
Definition.

#28
To Be Brave Is To Love Unconditionally
Without Expecting Anything In Return.

#29
Once You Learn To Accept And Love Them
For Who They Are, You Subconsciously Learn
To Love Yourself Unconditionally.

#30
The Source Of Love Is Deep In Us And We
Can Help Others Realize A Lot Of Happiness.
One Word, One Action, One Thought Can
Reduce Another Person's Suffering And Bring
That Person Joy.

#31
The More You Are Motivated By Love, The
More Fearless And Free Your Action Will Be.

#32
We Come To Love Not By Finding A Perfect Person, But By Learning To See An Imperfect Person Perfectly.

#33
The Heart Has Its Reasons Which Reason Knows Not.

#34
A Life Of Love Is One Of Continual Growth, Where The Doors And Windows Of Experience Are Always Open To The Wonder And Magic That Life Offers.

#35
Love Is The Voice Under All Silences, The Hope Which Has No Opposite In Fear; The Strength So Strong Mere Force Is Feebleness: The Truth More First Than Sun, More Last Than Star.

#36
The Heart Has Its Own Language. The Heart Knows A Hundred Thousand Ways To Speak.

#37
True Love Is Eternal, Infinite, And Always Like Itself. It Is Equal And Pure, Without Violent Demonstrations: It Is Seen With White Hairs And Is Always Young In The Heart.

#38
When You Love Someone, You Love The Whole Person, Just As He Or She Is, And Not As You Would Like Them To Be.

#39
Love Is An Endless Mystery, Because There Is No Reasonable Cause That Could Explain It.

#40
That's When You Know You Love Someone… When You Can't Experience Anything Without Wishing The Other Person Was There To See It, Too.

#41
Lovers Don't Finally Meet Somewhere. They Are In Each Other All Along.

#42
To Love Is To Recognize Yourself In Another.

#43
Deep Love Means You Put Your Ego Aside And Accept Unconditionally. It Means You're A Little Foolish. It Means You're Living.

#44
Love Is A Rebellious Bird That Nobody Can Tame.

#45
You Don't Love Someone Because Of Their Looks Or Their Clothes Or Their Car. You Love Them Because They Sing A Song Only Your Heart Can Understand.

#46
Love Is An Untamed Force. When We Try To Control It, It Destroys Us. When We Try To Imprison It, It Enslaves Us. When We Try To Understand It, It Leaves Us Feeling Lost And Confused.

#47
You Yourself, As Much As Anybody In The Entire Universe, Deserve Your Love And Affection.

#48
Love Does Not Dominate; It Cultivates.

#49
Immature Love Says: 'I Love You Because I Need You.' Mature Love Says 'I Need You Because I Love You.

#50
Love Recognizes No Barriers. It Jumps Hurdles, Leaps Fences, Penetrates Walls To Arrive At Its Destination Full Of Hope.

#51
Don't Brood. Get On With Living And Loving. You Don't Have Forever.

#52
Love Is When You Meet Someone Who Tells You Something New About Yourself.

#53
The Greatest Happiness Of Life Is The Deep Feelings That We Are Being Loved; Loved For Being Ourselves, Or Rather, Loved In Spite Of Ourselves.

#54
Love Is When You Meet That One Person Who Tells You Something New About Yourself That You Never Saw.

#55
One Day Someone Will Walk Into Your Life And Make You Realize How It Feels To Live A True Love Story.

#56
First Love And Last Love Both Are Important For You First Love Changes Your Nature While Last Love Changes Your Life.

#57
Love Isn't Finding A Perfect Person. It's Seeing An Imperfect Person Perfectly.

#58
Let The Beauty Of What You Love Be What You Do.

#59
Love Waits For All Of Us Quietly In That Place Where No One Is Looking.

#60
Being Deeply Loved By Someone Gives You Strength While Loving Someone Deeply Gives You Courage.

#61
Love Is Putting Up With Someone's Bad Qualities Because They Somehow Complete You.

#62
True Love Is Giving Someone All Your Attention When Ten Other People Are Asking For It.

#63
For Small Creatures Such As We, The Vastness Is Bearable Only Through Love.

#64
Love As A Power Can Go Anywhere. It Isn't Sentimental. It Doesn't Have To Be Pretty, Yet It Doesn't Deny Pain.

#65
To Be Brave Is To Love Someone Unconditionally, Without Expecting Anything In Return.

#66
Love Cures People – Both The Ones Who Give It And The Ones Who Receive It.

#67
You Never Lose By Loving. You Always Lose
By Holding Back.

#68
Love Is The Emblem Of Eternity; It Confounds
All Notion Of Time; Effaces All Memory Of A
Beginning, All Fear Of An End.

#69
Do What You Love, And You Will Find The
Way To Get It Out To The World.

#70
Love Is A Great Master. It Teaches Us To Be
What We Never Were.

#71
Love Is The Strange Bewilderment Which
Overtakes One Person On Account Of Another
Person.

#72

Everything That You Love, You Will Eventually Lose, But In The End, Love Will Return In A Different Form.

#73

Love Makes Your Soul Crawl Out From Its Hiding Place.

#74

Love Is More Than A Noun – It Is A Verb; It Is More Than A Feeling – It Is Caring, Sharing, Helping, Sacrificing.

#75

The Greatest Thing You'll Ever Learn Is To Love And Be Loved In Return.

#76

Love's Greatest Gift Is Its Ability To Make Everything It Touches Sacred.

#77
One Word Frees Us Of All The Weight And
Pain Of Life: That Word Is Love.

#78
Love Is The Expansion Of Two Natures In
Such Fashion That Each Include The Other,
Each Is Enriched By The Other.

#79
Unless You Love Someone, Nothing Else
Makes Sense.

#80
Each Time You Love, Love As Deeply As If It
Were Forever – Only, Nothing Is Eternal.

#81
Love Does Not Begin And End The Way We
Seem To Think It Does. Love Is A Battle; Love
Is A War; Love Is A Growing Up.

#82
Find The Person Who Will Love You Because
Of Your Differences And Not In Spite Of Them
And You Have Found A Lover For Life.

#83
Close Your Eyes For A While. The Image That
Conjures Is Your Soulmate. Don't Pause,
Rush And Say What You Feel. After All Time
And Tide For None Wait.

#84
A Soulmate Is The One Person Whose Love Is
Powerful Enough To Motivate You To Meet
Your Soul, To Do The Emotional Work Of Self-
Discovery, Of Awakening.

#85
Some Souls Just Understand Each Other
Upon Meeting.

#86
Giving Someone A Piece Of Your Soul Is
Better Than Giving A Piece Of Your Heart.
Because Souls Are Eternal.

#87
To Love And To Be Loved Is To Feel The Sun From Both Sides.

#88
The Best Love Is The Kind That Awakens The Soul; That Makes Us Reach For More, That Plants The Fire In Our Hearts And Brings Peace To Our Minds. That's What I Hope To Give You Forever.

#89
You Come To Love Not By Finding The Perfect Person, But By Seeing An Imperfect Person Perfectly.

#90
The Best Things In Life Can Never Be Kept; They Must Be Given Away. A Smile, A Kiss, And Love.

#91
Love Is But The Discovery Of Ourselves In Another, And The Delight In The Recognition.

#92
True Love Comes Quietly, Without Banners Or Flashing Lights. If You Hear Bells, Get Your Ears Checked.

#93
Love Is What Makes The Ride Worthwhile.

#94
A Woman Knows The Face Of The Man She Loves As A Sailor Knows The Open Sea.

#95
We Love Because It's The Only True Adventure.

#96
Love And Kindness Are Never Wasted. They Always Make A Difference. They Bless The One Who Receives Them, And They Bless You, The Giver.

#97
Where There Is Love There Is Life.

#98
Just In Case You Have Forgotten Today: You Matter. You Are Loved. You Are Worthy. You Are Magical.

#99
And In The End, The Love You Take, Is Equal To The Love You Make.

#100
Patience Is The Mark Of True Love. If You Truly Love Someone, You Will Be More Patient With That Person.

#101
Better To Have Lost And Loved Than Never To Have Loved At All.

#102
Love Is Never Lost. If Not Reciprocated, It Will Flow Back And Soften And Purify The Heart.

#103
Love Is What You've Been Through With Somebody.

#104
To Love Is Nothing. To Be Loved Is Something. But To Love And Be Loved, That's Everything.

#105
All You Need Is Love. But A Little Chocolate Now And Then Doesn't Hurt.

#106
Love Is That Condition In Which The Happiness Of Another Person Is Essential To Your Own.

#107
Love Is A Fire. But Whether It Is Going To Warm Your Hearth Or Burn Down Your House, You Can Never Tell.

#108
Love Doesn't Just Sit There, Like A Stone, It Has To Be Made, Like Bread; Remade All The Time, Made New.

#109
Love Does Not Consist Of Gazing At Each Other, But In Looking Outward Together In The Same Direction.

#110
Two People In Love, Alone, Isolated From The World, That's Beautiful.

#111
We Loved With A Love That Was More Than Love.

#112
Nobody Has Ever Measured, Not Even Poets,
How Much The Heart Can Hold.

#113
We Love The Things We Love For What They
Are.

#114
When We Love, We Always Strive To Become
Better Than We Are. When We Strive To
Become Better Than We Are, Everything
Around Us Becomes Better Too.

#115
Love Is Like The Wind, You Can't See It But
You Can Feel It.

#116
When Someone Loves You, The Way They
Talk About You Is Different. You Feel Safe
And Comfortable.

#117
Love Looks Not With The Eyes, But With The Mind, And Therefore Is Winged Cupid Painted Blind.

#118
Love Is The Enchanted Dawn Of Every Heart.

#119
I Knew Why Love Was Always Described With Eternity. A Single Minute Stretched Out For Lifetimes.

#120
You Must Love In Such A Way That The Person You Love Feels Free.

#121
One Word Frees Us Of All The Weight And Pain In Life. That Word Is Love!

#122
The Beauty Of Your Life Is Predicated On The Richness Of Your Sensuality.

#123
The Beautiful Thing About Love Is That You Just Need To Plant It Once And Nurture It And It Shall Bloom Into Blossoms That Would Cover The Valleys.

#124
Love Asks Me No Questions, And Gives Me Endless Support.

#125
Love Understands Love; It Needs No Talk.

#126
There Can Be No Deep Disappointment Where There Is Not Deep Love.

#127
Love Grows By Giving. The Love We Give Away Is The Only Love We Keep. The Only Way To Retain Love Is To Give It Away.

#128
A Truly Sensual Woman Is The Kind Of Woman Only A Man With A Deep Soul Can Intoxicate And Satiate.

#129
Love Is Supposed To Be Based On Trust, And Trust On Love, It's Something Rare And Beautiful When People Can Confide In Each Other Without Fearing What The Other Person Will Think.

#130
A Flower Cannot Blossom Without Sunshine, And Man Cannot Live Without Love.

#131
You Know You're In Love When You Don't Want To Fall Asleep Because Reality Is Finally Better Than Your Dreams.

#132
Lots Of People Want To Ride With You In The Limo, But What You Want Is Someone Who Will Take The Bus With You When The Limo Breaks Down.

#133
The Only Thing We Never Get Enough Of Is Love; And The Only Thing We Never Give Enough Of Is Love.

#134
Life Without Love Is Like A Tree Without Blossoms Or Fruit.

#135
Keep Love In Your Heart. A Life Without It Is Like A Sunless Garden When The Flowers Are Dead.

#136
The Best And Most Beautiful Things In This World Cannot Be Seen Or Even Heard, But Must Be Felt With The Heart.

#137
You Know It's Love When All You Want Is
That Person To Be Happy, Even If You're Not
Part Of Their Happiness.

#138
Love Is Of All Passions The Strongest, For It
Attacks Simultaneously The Head, The Heart,
And The Senses.

#139
The Way To Love Anything Is To Realize That
It May Be Lost.

#140
When We Are In Love We Seem To
Ourselves Quite Different From What We
Were Before.

#141
Love Is Not About How Many Days, Weeks Or
Months You've Been Together, It's All About
How Much You Love Each Other Every Day.

#142
We Are Shaped And Fashioned By What We Love.

#143
Love Is A Friendship Set To Music.

#144
The Most Important Thing In Life Is To Learn How To Give Out Love, And To Let It Come In.

#145
Love Yourself First And Everything Else Falls Into Line. You Really Have To Love Yourself To Get Anything Done In This World.

#146
You Have Found True Love When You Realize That You Want To Wake Up Beside Your Love Every Morning Even When You Have Your Differences.

#147
Love Takes Off Masks That We Fear We Cannot Live Without And Know We Cannot Live Within.

#148
To The World You May Be One Person, But To One Person You Are The World.

#149
Love Is When The Other Person's Happiness Is More Important Than Your Own.

#150
Love Is The Crowning Grace Of Humanity, The Holiest Right Of The Soul, The Golden Link Which Binds Us.

#151
You Can't Blame Gravity For Falling In Love.

#152
We Are Born Of Love; Love Is Our Mother.

#153
Love Isn't Something You Find. Love Is Something That Finds You.

#154
Sometimes The Heart Sees What Is Invisible To The Eye.

#155
True Love Is Eternal, Infinite, And Always Like Itself.

#156
Let Us Always Meet Each Other With Smile, For The Smile Is The Beginning Of Love.

#157
A Woman Knows The Face Of The Man She Loves As A Sailor Knows The Open Sea.

#158
Love Is Friendship That Has Caught Fire. It Settles For Less Than Perfection And Makes Allowances For Human Weaknesses.

#159
Love Is When He Gives You A Piece Of Your Soul, That You Never Knew Was Missing.

#160
Love Is The Magician That Pulls Man Out Of His Own Hat.

#161
We Love But Once, For Once Only Are We Perfectly Equipped For Loving.

#162
The Greatest Happiness Of Life Is The Conviction That We Are Loved.

#163
Love Is An Act Of Endless Forgiveness, A Tender Look Which Becomes A Habit.

#164
Love Is Like A Friendship Caught On Fire. As Love Grows Older, Our Hearts Mature And Our Love Becomes As Coals, Deep-Burning And Unquenchable.

#165
Love Is Like A Beautiful Flower Which I May Not Touch, But Whose Fragrance Makes The Garden A Place Of Delight Just The Same.

#166
Suddenly We See That Love Costs All We Are, And Will Ever Be. Yet It Is Only Love Which Sets Us Free.

#167
Love Is A Game That Two Can Play And Both Win.

#168
Love Is A Force More Formidable Than Any Other. It Is Invisible – It Cannot Be Seen Or Measured, Yet It Is Powerful Enough To Transform You In A Moment, And Offer You More Joy Than Any Material Possession Could.

#169
I Have Found The Paradox, That If You Love Until It Hurts, There Can Be No More Hurt, Only More Love.

#170
Love Is Life. And If You Miss Love, You Miss Life.

#171
The Most Powerful Weapon On Earth Is The Human Soul On Fire.

#172
A Kiss Is A Lovely Trick Designed By Nature To Stop Speech When Words Become Superfluous.

#173
There Is No Limit To The Power Of Loving.

#174
Love Possesses Not Nor Will It Be Possessed,
For Love Is Sufficient Unto Love.

#175
Love Is A Smoke Made With The Fume Of
Sighs.

#176
Love And Compassion Are Necessities, Not
Luxuries. Without Them Humanity Cannot
Survive.

#177
Love Doesn't Make The World Go 'Round.
Love Is What Makes The Ride Worthwhile.

#178
We Love Life, Not Because We Are Used To
Living But Because We Are Used To Loving.

#179
To Love Oneself Is The Beginning Of A Lifelong Romance.

#180
The Best Thing To Hold Onto In Life Is Each Other.

#181
Love Is The Flower You've Got To Let Grow.

#182
Love Is Composed Of A Single Soul Inhabiting Two Bodies.

#183
Love Does Not Consist In Gazing At Each Other, But In Looking Outward Together In The Same Direction.

#184
The Heart Wants What It Wants - Or Else It
Does Not Care.

#185
Love Is An Irresistible Desire To Be Irresistibly
Desired.

#186
True Love Is Like Ghosts, Which Everyone
Talks About And Few Have Seen.

#187
A Gentle Heart Is Tied With An Easy Thread.

#188
If You Can Learn To Love Yourself And All
The Flaws, You Can Love Other People So
Much Better. And That Makes You So Happy.

#189
Love Is Stronger Than Death.

#190
To Good And True Love Fear Is Forever
Affixed.

#191
If You Wish To Be Loved, Love.

#192
Spread Love Everywhere You Go. Let No One
Ever Come To You Without Leaving Happier.

#193
Love Is The Only Reality And It Is Not A Mere
Sentiment. It Is The Ultimate Truth That Lies
At The Heart Of Creation.

#194
Stolen Kisses Are Always Sweetest.

#195
Love Is A Sacred Reserve Of Energy; It Is Like
The Blood Of Spiritual Evolution.

#196

The Hunger For Love Is Much More Difficult
To Remove Than The Hunger For Bread.

#197

Kindness In Words Creates Confidence.
Kindness In Thinking Creates Profoundness.
Kindness In Giving Creates Love.

#198

Love Cures People – Both The Ones Who
Give It And The Ones Who Receive It.

#199

Love Many Things, For Therein Lies The True
Strength, And Whosoever Loves Much
Performs Much, And Can Accomplish Much,
And What Is Done In Love Is Done Well.

#200

A Part Of Kindness Consists In Loving People
More Than They Deserve.

#201
Love Takes Off Masks That We Fear We
Cannot Live Without And Know We Cannot
Live Within.

#202
We Accept The Love We Think We Deserve.

#203
It Is Better To Be Hated For What You Are
Than To Be Loved For What You Are Not.

#204
Love All, Trust A Few, Do Wrong To None.

#205
Two Things You Will Never Have To Chase:
True Friends & True Love.

#206
There Is Never A Time Or Place For True
Love. It Happens Accidentally, In A Heartbeat,
In A Single Flashing, Throbbing Moment.

#207
So Long As We Love We Serve; So Long As We Are Loved By Others, I Would Almost Say That We Are Indispensable; And No Man Is Useless While He Has A Friend.

#208
We're All A Little Weird. And Life Is A Little Weird. And When We Find Someone Whose Weirdness Is Compatible With Ours, We Join Up With Them And Fall Into Mutually Satisfying Weirdness—And Call It Love—True Love.

#209
Love Never Dies A Natural Death. It Dies Because We Don't Know How To Replenish Its Source. It Dies Of Blindness And Errors And Betrayals. It Dies Of Illness And Wounds; It Dies Of Weariness, Of Witherings, Of Tarnishings.

#210
The Real Lover Is The Man Who Can Thrill You By Kissing Your Forehead Or Smiling Into Your Eyes Or Just Staring Into Space.

#211

Just When You Think It Can't Get Any Worse, It Can. And Just When You Think It Can't Get Any Better, It Can.

#212

He's Not Perfect. You Aren't Either, And The Two Of You Will Never Be Perfect. But If He Can Make You Laugh At Least Once, Causes You To Think Twice, And If He Admits To Being Human And Making Mistakes, Hold Onto Him And Give Him The Most You Can.

#213

The One You Love And The One Who Loves You Are Never, Ever The Same Person.

#214

One Is Loved Because One Is Loved. No Reason Is Needed For Loving.

#215

Love Is Needing Someone. Love Is Putting Up With Someone's Bad Qualities Because They Somehow Complete You.

#216
You Are An Unlimited Being Filled With Infinite Possibility, With The Power To Be, Do Or Create Anything That You Desire In Your Life.

#217
Never Love Anyone Who Treats You Like You're Ordinary.

#218
You Don't Love Because: You Love Despite; Not For The Virtues, But Despite The Faults.

#219
Every Heart Sings A Song, Incomplete, Until Another Heart Whispers Back. Those Who Wish To Sing Always Find A Song. At The Touch Of A Lover, Everyone Becomes A Poet.

#220
We Loved With A Love That Was More Than Love.

#221
This Is A Good Sign, Having A Broken Heart. It Means We Have Tried For Something.

#222
What's Meant To Be Will Always Find A Way.

#223
They Say A Person Needs Just Three Things To Be Truly Happy In This World: Someone To Love, Something To Do, And Something To Hope For.

#224
No Relationship Is Perfect, Ever. There Are Always Some Ways You Have To Bend, To Compromise, To Give Something Up In Order To Gain Something Greater.

#225
Love Is So Short, Forgetting Is So Long.

#226
The Very Essence Of Romance Is Uncertainty.

#227
Man May Have Discovered Fire, But Women Discovered How To Play With It.

#228
If You Love Somebody, Let Them Go, For If They Return, They Were Always Yours. If They Don't, They Never Were.

#229
Love Is A Fire. But Whether It Is Going To Warm Your Hearth Or Burn Down Your House, You Can Never Tell.

#230
More Smiling, Less Worrying. More Compassion, Less Judgment. More Blessed, Less Stressed. More Love, Less Hate.

#231
Be Careful Of Love. It'll Twist Your Brain
Around And Leave You Thinking Up Is Down
And Right Is Wrong.

#232
Be The Reason Someone Smiles. Be The
Reason Someone Feels Loved And Believes
In The Goodness In People.

#233
If You Like Her, If She Makes You Happy, And
If You Feel Like You Know Her, Then Don't Let
Her Go.

#234
A Woman's Heart Should Be So Hidden In
God That A Man Has To Seek Him Just To
Find Her.

#235
The Most Painful Thing Is Losing Yourself In
The Process Of Loving Someone Too Much,
And Forgetting That You Are Special Too.

#236
It Is A Curious Thought, But It Is Only When You See People Looking Ridiculous That You Realize Just How Much You Love Them.

#237
When The Power Of Love Overcomes The Love Of Power, The World Will Know Peace.

#238
What Is Love? I Have Met In The Streets A Very Poor Young Man Who Was In Love. His Hat Was Old, His Coat Worn, The Water Passed Through His Shoes And The Stars Through His Soul.

#239
The Man Of Knowledge Must Be Able Not Only To Love His Enemies But Also To Hate His Friends.

#240
The Greater The Love, The Greater The Tragedy When It's Over.

#241
If You Gave Someone Your Heart And They
Died, Did They Take It With Them? Did You
Spend The Rest Of Forever With A Hole Inside
You That Couldn't Be Filled?

#242
Never Close Your Lips To Those Whom You
Have Already Opened Your Heart.

#243
Things We Lose Have A Way Of Coming Back
To Us In The End, If Not Always In The Way
We Expect.

#244
It's Not The Face, But The Expressions On It.
It's Not The Voice, But What You Say. It's Not
How You Look In That Body, But The Thing
You Do With It. You Are Beautiful.

#245
Any Fool Can Be Happy. It Takes A Man With
Real Heart To Make Beauty Out Of The Stuff
That Makes Us Weep.

#246
You Know, When It Works, Love Is Pretty
Amazing. It's Not Overrated. There's A Reason
For All Those Songs.

#247
Love Is Not Affectionate Feeling, But A Steady
Wish For The Loved Person's Ultimate Good
As Far As It Can Be Obtained.

#248
We Waste Time Looking For The Perfect
Lover, Instead Of Creating The Perfect Love.

#249
Love Is An Untamed Force. When We Try To
Control It, It Destroys Us. When We Try To
Imprison It, It Enslaves Us. When We Try To
Understand It, It Leaves Us Feeling Lost And
Confused.

#250
You Couldn't Relive Your Life, Skipping The Awful Parts, Without Losing What Made It Worthwhile. You Had To Accept It As A Whole--Like The World, Or The Person You Loved.

#251
Happiness Is Only Real When Shared.

#252
You Can't Measure The Mutual Affection Of Two Human Beings By The Number Of Words They Exchange.

#253
Letting Go Doesn't Mean That You Don't Care About Someone Anymore. It's Just Realizing That The Only Person You Really Have Control Over Is Yourself.

#254
Sometimes It's A Form Of Love Just To Talk
To Somebody That You Have Nothing In
Common With And Still Be Fascinated By
Their Presence.

#255
Every One Of Us Is, In The Cosmic
Perspective, Precious. If A Human Disagrees
With You, Let Him Live. In A Hundred Billion
Galaxies, You Will Not Find Another.

#256
Art And Love Are The Same Thing: It's The
Process Of Seeing Yourself In Things That Are
Not You.

#257
Respect Was Invented To Cover The Empty
Place Where Love Should Be.

#258
Happiness Is Holding Someone In Your Arms
And Knowing You Hold The Whole World.

#259
Love Can Change A Person The Way A
Parent Can Change A Baby- Awkwardly, And
Often With A Great Deal Of Mess.

#260
It Is Easy To Love People In Memory; The
Hard Thing Is To Love Them When They Are
There In Front Of You.

#261
You Know How They Say You Only Hurt The
Ones You Love? Well, It Works Both Ways.

#262
Trust Your Heart If The Seas Catch Fire, Live
By Love Though The Stars Walk Backward.

#263
The More One Judges, The Less One Loves.

#264

Sorrow Is How We Learn To Love. Your Heart Isn't Breaking. It Hurts Because It's Getting Larger. The Larger It Gets; The More Love It Holds.

#265

It Takes Courage To Love, But Pain Through Love Is The Purifying Fire Which Those Who Love Generously Know.

#266

When Someone Is In Your Heart, They're Never Truly Gone. They Can Come Back To You, Even At Unlikely Times.

#267

Don't Cry Over Someone Who Wouldn't Cry Over You.

#268

Sometimes Love Means Letting Go When You Want To Hold On Tighter.

#269
Absence Diminishes Small Loves And Increases Great Ones, As The Wind Blows Out The Candle And Fans The Bonfire.

#270
When You Trip Over Love, It Is Easy To Get Up. But When You Fall In Love, It Is Impossible To Stand Again.

#271
True Love Is Usually The Most Inconvenient Kind.

#272
The Things We Love Destroy Us Every Time, Lad. Remember That.

#273
The Course Of True Love Never Did Run Smooth.

#274
To Lose Balance Sometimes For Love Is Part Of Living A Balanced Life.

#275
This Is What We Call Love. When You Are Loved, You Can Do Anything In Creation. When You Are Loved, There's No Need At All To Understand What's Happening, Because Everything Happens Within You.

#276
Sometimes You Don't Need A Goal In Life, You Don't Need To Know The Big Picture. You Just Need To Know What You're Going To Do Next!

#277
Don't Waste Your Love On Somebody, Who Doesn't Value It.

#278
For Where All Love Is, The Speaking Is Unnecessary.

#279
We Are Who We Are, Because Of Those We Choose To Love And Because Of Those Who Love Us.

#280
Love Is How You Stay Alive, Even After You Are Gone.

#281
So It's True, When All Is Said And Done, Grief Is The Price We Pay For Love.

#282
There Is Nothing More Truly Artistic Than To Love People.

#283
Despite Your Best Efforts, People Are Going To Be Hurt When It's Time For Them To Be Hurt.

#284
That's What People Do Who Love You. They Put Their Arms Around You And Love You When You're Not So Lovable.

#285
Do What You Love, Love What You Do, And With All Your Heart Give Yourself To It.

#286
Let Yourself Be Drawn By The Stronger Pull Of That Which You Truly Love.

#287
Goodbyes Are Only For Those Who Love With Their Eyes. Because For Those Who Love With Heart And Soul There Is No Such Thing As Separation.

#288
We Are Told That People Stay In Love Because Of Chemistry, Or Because They Remain Intrigued With Each Other, Because Of Many Kindnesses, Because Of Luck. But Part Of It Has Got To Be Forgiveness And Gratefulness.

#289
True Love Is Not So Much A Matter Of Romance As It Is A Matter Of Anxious Concern For The Well-Being Of One's Companion.

#290
Love Has Nothing To Do With What You Are Expecting To Get - Only With What You Are Expecting To Give - Which Is Everything.

#291
There Is Always Something Left To Love.

#292

I Told You. You Don't Love Someone Because Of Their Looks Or Their Clothes Or Their Car. You Love Them Because They Sing A Song Only Your Heart Can Understand.

#293

The Heart Is The Toughest Part Of The Body. Tenderness Is In The Hands.

#294

True Love Comes Quietly, Without Banners Or Flashing Lights. If You Hear Bells, Get Your Ears Checked.

#295

Love Is The Extremely Difficult Realization That Something Other Than Oneself Is Real.

#296

Someday You'll Find Someone Special Again. People Who've Been In Love Once Usually Do. It's In Their Nature.

#297
Love Is A Better Master Than Duty.

#298
If You Spend Your Time Hoping Someone Will Suffer The Consequences For What They Did To Your Heart, Then You're Allowing Them To Hurt You A Second Time In Your Mind.

#299
The Scariest Thing About Distance Is That You Don't Know Whether They'll Miss You Or Forget You.

#300
Accept The Things To Which Fate Binds You, And Love The People With Whom Fate Brings You Together, But Do So With All Your Heart.

#301
Love And Compassion Are Necessities, Not Luxuries. Without Them, Humanity Cannot Survive.

#302
The Fate Of Your Heart Is Your Choice And
No One Else Gets A Vote.

#303
We Are All Worthy Of One Another.

#304
Anyone Who Loves In The Expectation Of
Being Loved In Return Is Wasting Their Time.

#305
When You Love Someone, You Say Their
Name Different. Like It's Safe Inside Your
Mouth.

#306
The Only Thing More Unthinkable Than
Leaving Was Staying; The Only Thing More
Impossible Than Staying Was Leaving.

#307
Love Sucks. Sometimes It Feels Good. Sometimes It's Just Another Way To Bleed.

#308
Love Recognizes No Barriers. It Jumps Hurdles, Leaps Fences, Penetrates Walls To Arrive At Its Destination Full Of Hope.

#309
Some People Feel Like They Don't Deserve Love. They Walk Away Quietly Into Empty Spaces, Trying To Close The Gaps Of The Past.

#310
Whenever You Are Confronted With An Opponent. Conquer Him With Love.

#311
When In A Relationship, A Real Man Doesn't Make His Woman Jealous Of Others, He Makes Others Jealous Of His Woman.

#312
The Strongest Love Is The Love That Can
Demonstrate Its Fragility.

#313
Remember That The Best Relationship Is One
In Which Your Love For Each Other Exceeds
Your Need For Each Other.

#314
To Love Someone Means To See Them As
God Intended Them.

#315
Love Makes You Want To Be A Better Man.
But Maybe Love, Real Love, Also Gives You
Permission To Just Be The Man You Are.

#316
He's Not Your Prince Charming If He Doesn't
Make Sure You Know That You're His
Princess.

#317
There Are Memories That Time Does Not
Erase... Forever Does Not Make Loss
Forgettable, Only Bearable.

#318
When You Love Someone You Let Them Take
Care Of You.

#319
You Will Never Be Able To Escape From Your
Heart. So It's Better To Listen To What It Has
To Say.

#320
If You Truly Want To Be Respected By People
You Love, You Must Prove To Them That You
Can Survive Without Them.

#321
There Is Love In Holding And There Is Love In
Letting Go.

#322
The Power Of Finding Beauty In The
Humblest Things Makes Home Happy And Life
Lovely.

#323
Love Is Our True Destiny. We Do Not Find The
Meaning Of Life By Ourselves Alone - We Find
It With Another.

#324
You'll Never Be Able To Find Yourself If
You're Lost In Someone Else.

#325
There Is No Intensity Of Love Or Feeling That
Does Not Involve The Risk Of Crippling Hurt. It
Is A Duty To Take This Risk, To Love And
Feel Without Defense Or Reserve.

#326
If You Don't Receive Love From The Ones
Who Are Meant To Love You, You Will Never
Stop Looking For It.

#327
Ah, What Happiness It Is To Be With People Who Are All Happy, To Press Hands, Press Cheeks, Smile Into Eyes.

#328
There Comes A Time In Your Life When You Have To Choose To Turn The Page, Write Another Book Or Simply Close It.

#329
Sometimes It Takes A Heartbreak To Shake Us Awake & Help Us See We Are Worth So Much More Than We're Settling For.

#330
There Could Have Been No Two Hearts So Open, No Tastes So Similar, No Feelings So In Unison.

#331
People Should Fall In Love With Their Eyes Closed.

#332
Where There Is Great Love, There Are Always Miracles.

#333
To Love Is To Recognize Yourself In Another.

#334
Life Is Funny. Things Change, People Change, But You Will Always Be You, So Stay True To Yourself And Never Sacrifice Who You Are For Anyone.

#335
Don't Sacrifice Yourself Too Much, Because If You Sacrifice Too Much There's Nothing Else You Can Give And Nobody Will Care For You.

#336
Be The One Who Nurtures And Builds. Be The One Who Has An Understanding And A Forgiving Heart One Who Looks For The Best In People. Leave People Better Than You Found Them.

#337
Choose Your Love. Love Your Choice.

#338
True Love Begins When Nothing Is Looked
For In Return.

#339
If You Love Deeply, You're Going To Get Hurt
Badly. But It's Still Worth It.

#340
Sometimes We Love With Nothing More Than
Hope. Sometimes We Cry With Everything
Except Tears.

#341
When You Love Someone, It's Never Over.
You Move On, Because You Have To But You
Take Them With You In Your Heart.

#342

If You Love Something So Much Let It Go. If It Comes Back It Was Meant To Be; If It Doesn't It Never Was.

#343

You Can Live Your Whole Life Not Realizing That What You're Looking For Is Right In Front Of You.

#344

It's One Thing To Fall In Love. It's Another To Feel Someone Else Fall In Love With You, And To Feel A Responsibility Toward That Love.

#345

Oh, Love Isn't There To Make Us Happy. I Believe It Exists To Show Us How Much We Can Endure.

#346

Love Wins, Love Always Wins.

#347
Life Is A Gift. Don't Forget To Live It.

#348
Love Doesn't Mean Anything If You're Not Willing To Make A Commitment, And You Have To Think Not Only About What You Want, But About What He Wants. Not Just Now, But In The Future.

#349
When You Love You Wish To Do Things For. You Wish To Sacrifice For. You Wish To Serve.

#350
Love, Like Fire, Goes Out Without Fuel.

#351
If A Man Hasn't What's Necessary To Make A Woman Love Him, It's His Fault, Not Hers.

#352
When You Feel Someone Else's Pain And Joy
As Powerfully As If It Were Your Own, Then
You Know You Really Loved Them.

#353
That's When You Know For Sure Somebody
Loves You. They Figure Out What You Need
And They Give It To You -- Without You
Asking.

#354
If You're Smart, You Care. And If You Care,
You Love.

#355
Hope For Love, Pray For Love, Wish For Love,
Dream For Love…But Don't Put Your Life On
Hold Waiting For Love.

#356
The Only Way Love Can Last A Lifetime Is If
It's Unconditional. The Truth Is This: Love Is
Not Determined By The One Being Loved But
Rather By The One Choosing To Love.

#357
Love Is A Promise, Love Is A Souvenir, Once Given Never Forgotten, Never Let It Disappear.

#358
Love Is Always Open Arms. If You Close Your Arms About Love You Will Find That You Are Left Holding Only Yourself.

#359
Falling In Love You Remain A Child; Rising In Love You Mature. By And By Love Becomes Not A Relationship, It Becomes A State Of Your Being. Not That You Are In Love - Now You Are Love.

#360
It Is Better To Lose Your Pride With Someone You Love Rather Than To Lose That Someone You Love With Your Useless Pride.

#361
You Know Someone's Right For You When The Things They Don't Have To Say Are Even More Important Than The Things They Do.

#362
Looking At Beauty In The World, Is The First Step Of Purifying The Mind.

#363
When God Knows You're Ready For The Responsibility Of Commitment, He'll Reveal The Right Person Under The Right Circumstances.

#364
Love Is The Only Force Capable Of Transforming An Enemy To A Friend.

#365
You call it madness, but I call it love.

Please Leave A Review!

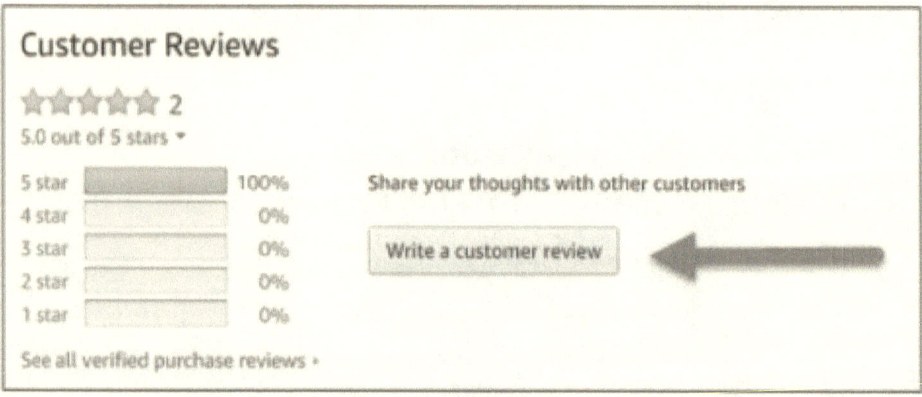

I would be incredibly thankful if you take just 60 seconds to write a brief review on Amazon, even if it is just a few positive words.

Conclusion

I hope you have gained happiness, love and a sense of wanting from the quotes you have read in this book. My aim with this book was to help anyone that just needed to have just a few positive loving words each day in their life to help them become the best version of themselves.

If you can please spare 60 seconds to leave a positive review on this book so I can help even more people with the positive words found inside.